YOU DECIDE
FIVE BELIEFS THAT CHANGED MY LIFE

YOU DECIDE
FIVE BELIEFS THAT CHANGED
MY LIFE

KNUTE LARSON

THE CHAPEL
AKRON, OH

Contents

Acknowledgements

The initiative and sponsorship for this book came through the gracious kindness of Paul Martin, a unique and generous friend of Akron, Ohio, who urged me to write down the most important beliefs from my time leading The Chapel.

I am thankful.

Also to Thomas Bacher, of The University of Akron Press, a cordial and excellent publisher and editor.

The five beliefs that I have written about have been taught and discussed many times at The Chapel in Akron and Green, Ohio. I acknowledge with deep gratitude the love and kinship I have found there.

The last is first: I am so grateful to God who first had these texts written, and for providing me with the adventure of my life.

Introduction

By the very nature of what a belief is, no one can be forced to believe something.

We can believe things that do not make sense, or that contradict what seems absolutely true, of course.

But clearly you and I both decide what we will believe.

For forty-two satisfying years, I have given my life to try to help people at least look into the most important issues of life, and to see what the Bible says about these.

Then they decide what to believe.

Sadly, many do little research, often embracing urban legends or stuff they Googled at random.

This book is the story of how one person grappled with five of the most serious personal issues of life:

- pain, and how it relates to a sovereign God ;
- forgiveness, and how to receive the love of a generous Lord;
- the daily walk of a believer, and what it means to cooperate with God, so all of life has integration with faith;
- wisdom choices, and the healthy freedom God offers us; and
- attitude, and why gratitude is everything.

After you go with me to these huge change points in my life, you decide what you want for yourself.

YOU DECIDE.

I

There Is a God

I was at the church I loved when I was called to the phone in the cloak room near the sanctuary. The call was from the hospital—my sister had been rushed there after falling off a horse at my father's little farm.

Nan, age 14, fell off the horse as it rushed back to the barn. She hit her head on a rock, and never regained any consciousness. I drove to the hospital, 17 and horrified.

She was 14, in a coma, with no hope.

The death was awful—a horse that had been traded for a used car. A Father's Day that saw her visiting my father who lived at this little house in the country with his new wife, because of the divorce five years before.

All the irony.

Both my mother and father would blame themselves, and I would blame God.

Maybe the real blame belongs to the horse, part of a groaning creation.

And my anger toward God picked right up there, continuing the great question marks at ages 10 through 12 when I had watched my parents fight and separate and ultimately divorce.

If marriage is communication, communication, communication, they majored on independence, autonomy, busyness. They drifted and began repelling each other.

They were the nicest of people. I still would say I have met few people as kind as my mother or as gentle as my dad, and yet I do remember with immediate clarity my standing between them to stop them from yelling at each other.

That is no place for a ten-year-old, and neither is death any place for a 17-year-old. Or for any of us.

I remember after that tragedy even asking what the point of prayer was since "God is going to do what He wishes anyway."

And this is no pity party—I know that many people have abandoned the search for meaning in life because of their own personal tragedies. Or because nothing seems to make sense as to an eternal plan.

Or because they have heard someone's feeble attempt to explain the ways of a sovereign God—like explaining gravity or the conception of a human life, we have no way to talk about the miracle part.

My Change Point

It was during these troubled times that the beauty of a Psalm of honesty jumped out and grabbed my heart. I have slept on this verse and reached for it with my emotions many times.

It is so clear.

> *But I trust in you, oh Lord.*
> *I say, "You are my God."*
> *My times are in your hands.*
> Psalm 31:14, 15

It is a rock solid foundation for a life and also a soft pillow to sleep on.

It does not explain the wars overseas or the wars in the inner-city or in my own personal heart. It does not explain why some people do drugs and others cheat on their income tax. It does not satisfy me about why that horse was allowed to run so quickly back to the barn and leap over those rocks, causing my vivacious sister, captain of the cheerleaders in eighth grade, to fall off the back of the horse.

But it does tell me that my life can connect to God and rest in His magnificent power.

And allow Him to do the work of God while I do my small job.

I have learned also to try to accept that even my sister's and mother's times were in His sovereign hands. That is hard.

Nan was three years younger than me, so my brother and I were protecting and teasing her regularly. I can see her immediately right now running toward our house and Baby Doll, her Dachshund, who was scampering down the street toward her.

And our mother never quite worked through that tragedy. I do not think it is possible for a mother about her child.

All one can do is try to be in our Lord's hands.

SOME TIMES ARE AWFUL

To understand any verse, we must see its context. The first part of Psalm 31 confronts us with the truth—certain times are awful.

> *I am in distress;*
> *my eyes grow weak with sorrow,*
> *my soul and my body with grief.*
> Psalm 31:9

While the Psalmist starts by saying he is trusting God—"In you, oh Lord, I have taken refuge"—he continues with some panic. He prays for leadership and strength—"Be my rock of refuge, a strong fortress to save me "(31:2).

But it is quickly clear that he is lonely and forsaken: "Free me from the trap that is set for me" (31:4).

It even says words Jesus would later voice on the cross: "Into your hand I commit my spirit; redeem me, oh Lord, the God of truth."

And then his complaints set in—the kind I had at age 17 and later when my mother died from the awful attack of cancer. She was 46, way too young.

She was the best interior decorator in Harrisburg, Pennsylvania, having done the governor's mansion and many others.

But cancer is relentless, as are the other enemies we all face.

The Psalmist complained like all of us do: "My life is consumed by anguish and my years by groaning" (31:10).

Loneliness is gray—dull, bland, foggy gray, and the Psalmist and those who knew God best had those days too. They knew what it is to feel totally deserted—that's the Psalmist in the first part of this hymn.

If being alone is a fact of geography, loneliness is a state of the mind.

And we have all been there, even in crowds.

Creation's Groaning

It sounds like Romans 8:21, where it says the whole creation keeps groaning as it waits for the day of the return of Jesus Christ to make things perfect again.

There are wars and plagues, cancer and weeds. And there will be until The End.

But that seems so far away at times.

And it's been so long since He said He would come back to judge the world and clean up this place.

The Psalmist sums it up in verse 13 when he says, "There is terror on every side" (31:13).

Maybe comedian–amateur theologian Bill Maher is right when he laughs about God or even speaks as if He does not exist.

People say it all the time: "If God is really God, why doesn't He do something about all the pain in the world?"

They especially mean theirs. Take it away!

God Remade in Our Image

We developed this picture of God that makes it look like He should relieve all aches. It's the kind of God we would really like.

It's the same God that the followers of Jehovah at the time of Jesus had. I mean there's no question that they thought the Messiah would come and take out the Romans. And when He instead taught about the heart and didn't use His hands to defeat the enemy, they set out to crucify Him.

It's the same God people expect to deliver them out of every trench or gully.

Where did we get that? Not from the Bible. Not from God's teachings about Himself.

But we usually prefer to define Him on our own terms. He's our Santa Claus in the sky. He's our "big man upstairs" who steps in to defend us from tragedy or even a fistfight. He rescues us.

We got these theories because we like them.

But the next few verses in the Psalm turn it for me.

SOME TIMES ARE AWFUL BUT WE CAN TRUST GOD

But I trust in you, O Lord;
I say, "You are my God."
Psalm 31:14

This is where the Psalmist tells us how we can switch from just staring at the awful events of life or even trusting in our own ways: "I trust in you, oh Lord; I say, You are my God."

Then he adds what gave me great peace, about being in God's hands.

That is a decision of trust, a response of worship. That is a place in life which has to continue every day, but a place where we start to trust God to be God and believe what He says about sovereignty.

If the Bible says anything it says God is ultimately in charge. He is sovereign Lord, which does not mean He likes what is happening.

The groaning of the earth includes the awfulness of people, including ourselves. The pain and the groaning include many, many bad things happening to many, many good people.

Rabbi Kushner asked with his bestseller years ago, *Why Do Bad Things Happen to Good People?* He reckoned that God was there, but maybe He can't do anything about some things.

He can, but He does often sit back. And life attacks, and we groan.

But we can trust. To trust God means to believe that in the anguish and horrors of life He is still God. And He will eventually make things right and do what is best.

The Awfulness

I have not heard any question more than the question, "Why?"

"Why did my child die?"

"Why would God allow that in my life right now?"

"Why me?" (Usually said after something bad happens, and very infrequently after something good.)

And rather well-meaning people have often given answers that border on emptiness. We feel like we have to answer.

At calling hours for my sister, one lady whom I would call a religious fundamentalist walked by my mom—I was standing right beside her in front of the casket—and explained, "Maybe this happened because your daughter would have grown up to be a prostitute, and so God took her home."

Even at age 17, I had enough nerve to say, "Please, keep moving."

In reality there is nothing to say to someone who has just experienced a horrible tragedy. There is no way that because some good came to one person when this happened, the one experiencing the pain will feel okay about it.

Neither should we even say, "We'll know why this happened someday!"

I'm not sure we will know.

I'm not sure when we get to heaven we really will have that famous "list of questions" that we say we're going to ask God someday.

We probably will just fall down at the feet of our Lord in awe.

There will not be a question and answer time. It will be a worship experience.

And we will know that we were wise and right to trust God during this life.

Indeed.

Our Options

We have choices. We either go through tragedy by ourselves or we go through trusting the God who says He can get us through. He walks alongside us.

We either decide to do it alone or we believe that it is good to wait upon the Lord, as Isaiah said.

In urging us to do that Isaiah explained, "The Lord is the everlasting God, the Creator of the ends of the earth. He will not grow tired or weary, and His understanding no one can fathom" (Isaiah 40:27, 28).

But then Isaiah adds the prescription that is a parallel to this great verse in Psalm 31: "He gives strength to the weary and increases the power of the weak…. Those who hope in the Lord will renew their strength."

He adds a beautiful picture that gets us through when we trust God: They will soar on wings like eagles; they will run and not grow weary, and they will walk and not be faint (Isaiah 40:31).

And sometimes we feel like the strength of God makes us fly like eagles we get through so swiftly. Sometimes we work hard—I just finished 25 years of mighty long weeks in Akron to try to help people and promote grace—and I think Isaiah means such running hard but not getting tired.

Other times the best we can do is take another step. Walk. But we do not faint.

And that too is the provision of God.

But only when we trust in God and put our times in His hands.

SOME TIMES ARE AWFUL BUT WE CAN TRUST GOD AND SEE OURSELVES IN HIS HANDS

My times are in your hands.
Psalm 31:15

That means obedience and trust. That means we don't understand everything and we don't expect to, but we believe that He is God who will triumph someday and work things together for good in our lives right now.

And I was wondering if you have decided to believe that.

That's much better than coming up with that popular theory that gets passed around, "It was meant to be."

Where did you get that?

Somebody passed that around on the Oprah show or somewhere in your ancestry. Some fatalist thought it up on his deathbed.

Some gambler said it when he lost a big pile of chips.

Some football coach said it at the end of a hard-fought game when he either won or lost. You can say it anytime!

It must have been "in the cards"!

Nonsense.

I mean it did happen. But our part is not to figure out why it happened or decide to rest in fatalism, but rather to rest in the sovereign promises of God.

To learn through pain. To trust Him in the darkest hours.

To know that this life is full of groaning and that we will walk through the valley of the shadow of death, as that famous Psalm 23 says.

But also to believe and feel that He is with us. I got that right from the Bible.

I got that from watching the New Testament believers like Peter and Paul trust God in prison or in huge pain. They were trying to obey and trust the sovereignty of God, so they could rest even in pain.

They felt like what they believed was true, that when you seek to follow God as best you can, to walk in His ways of Scripture, you can then believe that your life is not experiencing accidents as much as sovereignty, never outside the rule of God.

Paul's Last Words

Then you can somehow adopt the words of the famous Apostle Paul when he was in prison writing about his death which was to come in three or four months: "I am already being poured out like a drink offering, and the time has come for my departure" (II Timothy 4:6).

So he was about to die but he knew his times were in the hands of God. He even called death a departure, because his spirit-soul—the real Paul was not the body but the spirit-soul—

was about to leave what he sometimes called his tent, his human body. To depart. To make an exodus.

Not to quit or to cease existing, as some people teach.

So he rested easy there in the prison cell awaiting his execution.

Whoa!

And then he added the reason he felt this way: "I have fought the good fight, I finished the race, I have kept the faith" (II Timothy 4:7). He had put his life in the hands of God, no question.

He had trusted God and seen himself as a servant of God.

He even added hope for the future: "Now there is in store for me the crown of righteousness, which the Lord, the righteous judge, will award to me on that day—and not only to me, but also to all who have longed for His appearing" (II Timothy 4:8).

So Paul knew that he was going to go to heaven—this was not a "knock on wood" kind of hope. He knew that he would see Christ and even receive reward.

He rested in that.

His times were in God's hands.

Knowing for Sure

People are always saying, "I don't think you can know for sure about eternal life."

Perhaps you heard these words from the guy at the coffee shop, or at the cafeteria at school, or maybe from my grade school friend who taught me about how sex works in marriage, and he was all wrong.

It doesn't hurt to say to people sometimes, "Where did you get that?" when they tell you about Thomas Jefferson's decision—that God started the world rolling and then backed off. He's taking a nap. He's doing other things.

Maybe He's trying to find out if there are people on Mars.

Instead the Bible teaches that He is very actively involved in this world, but not in the way we would be if we were CEO.

But He is watching over His children, holding them in His hand, and giving them confidence that there's meaning to life.

So when the Psalmist realizes his confidence in God and that His times are in God's hands, he prays, "Let your face shine on your servant; save me in your unfailing love " (Psalm 31:16).

He even gives a promise for everyone today: "How great is your goodness, which you have stored up for those who fear you, which you bestow in the sight of men on those who take refuge in you. In the shelter of your presence you hide them from the intrigues of men" (Psalm 31:19, 20).

He sums up the whole Psalm for me and for all who walk through shadows when he says, "Be strong and take heart, all you who hope in the Lord" (Psalm 31:24).

Help at the Church

When my parents divorced, the church sort of waved good-bye, with a few flicks of the fingers. My parents left the church also, so I can't blame only the church.

And when my sister died I remember a man at church asking me how I was getting along about that, and I began to cry, and he immediately changed the subject to something related to sports so I would not keep crying.

We just didn't know how to deal with it in the context of our faith. Or at least churches neglected that so easily.

So for 40 years as a senior pastor—25 almost 26 in Akron—I have pushed hard for groups and individual care for those who grieve and also for those who split from each other. Certainly our counselors in our groups have done everything possible to try to heal marriages that were breaking up, but we have also tried to provide places of healing when those storms hit.

Our weekly Divorce Recovery workshops have been well received. People from all over the region hear a talk on forgiveness or love or next steps, then gather in smaller caring groups to discuss.

The Grief Share program has been led by an innovator in the area of expressing sorrow and seeking strength. Even funeral homes have urged their clients to attend.

And I always urge people to place themselves in the hand of God. To give their times to Him. To trust Him from the inside out.

My Mother's Departure

I remember so clearly the last Christmas we celebrated with my mother. We knew death would be early in the calendar year.

On a Christmas morning, she shuffled her 70 pounds of weakness into the living room where we tried to give Christmas gifts. This would be the last she would see. We gave her new slippers.

And inside we all knew that what we were celebrating at Christmas, the coming of Jesus Christ into a world of pain, was why we could have hope also.

Her funeral would be called, "A Witness to the Resurrection." That's based on the death and resurrection of Jesus Christ. There is hope.

I don't know how people do it without that confidence that our times are in God's hands. And that our eternity is in His plans.

I do know how because I have led many of those funeral services. We just avoid thinking about where the real person is right now. We beat around the bush a little.

In plain terms, we call for people to trust Christ themselves, to honor His Word about resurrection and hope, without saying anything about the person whose body lies in the casket and whose spirit-soul is somewhere or other.

We hold out hope that the person did indeed place faith in Christ at the end. They could have.

How to Finish Strong

I was running in a 10K race and losing heart. I don't run fast, but I've always jogged with a fanaticism taught by my dad who had us running in first grade. We drank wheat germ after the jog and then went to school.

But in this race I was losing ground and nothing seemed to come. Every would-be athlete knows what it means, and so do the big guys. Even LeBron has those days.

I pulled hard and saw a huge hill in front of us, and I was getting ready to quit for the first time in my life.

An old man passed me on my right—he had to be 90 or 190. He had a bottle of honey in one hand and water in the other, and it was discouraging.

Then a woman passed me on my left. I'm not a chauvinist, but I didn't want this woman beating me in this race. I got ready to pull over to the side.

As another person began to pass me I motioned to him and toward the hill, "It's all yours.

"I'm quitting."

This stranger did not want me to do that. "Come on," he said, "run with me."

I don't know how much was adrenaline and how much was pure ego, but I tried. I started pulling for it. It—whatever "it" is—began to come.

"Lean over," he said, "take shorter steps up hills."

I leaned over and took shorter steps.

My times were in this runner's hands.

We ran together the rest of the race. I even remember saying to him, "Tell me I can do it."

"You can do it," he said automatically.

"You're just saying that," I laughed.

But we made it to the end. In fact, as I recall, we sprinted together the last 150 yards. Everyone had already gone home, but it felt good and we finished strong.

And I think about it for all of life: "Lean over; take shorter steps."

Don't be a big deal. Humble yourself. Put your times in the hands of God.

Trust Him, not yourself.

"Take shorter steps." Just go a day at a time. Maybe an hour at a time.

Maybe do the next thing you're supposed to do. Do what's right.

Read a Psalm and go to bed.

Make a phone call and put it behind you.

Say a prayer and decide that God has to do the God work and you can simply trust and see yourself in His hands. It's the way to live.

Our job is not to figure out what is the will of God or what He hopes we do next, but our job is to figure out what we should do next. To make wise decisions.

To do it all the while knowing our times are in His hands, and therefore we should obey Him.

This changed my heart from an angry young man to a trusting soul.

When we trust God like that, we are not victims of chance. We don't act like fatalism is our destiny.

We believe God is moving in the affairs of life in a way we cannot understand, but we can believe.

And we are in His hands.

A good place to be for sure.

YOU DECIDE.

II

There Is a Way

I've heard it 100 times. At least many.

"We do know all roads lead up the same mountain."

Do we know that? Where did that pastor get that before he said it to me? He was one of many.

I remember having a new friend say to me, "There are many saviors, we all know."

I asked with grace, "Where did you get that?"

He wasn't sure, but that's what he had always believed. And he said he was planning to go the rest of the way with that on his heart.

Perhaps one of the most dangerous tendencies we have in life is to live by theories that are untested, untried, even untrue.

If it's an arithmetic formula, and we have been taught that two and two is five, we'll probably get contradicted enough that we will look it up and find out where we got that.

If it's a medical theory, and we've been taught that certain poisons aren't so bad, we may get our opinion reversed in the hospital.

But if it's a theological issue, and nothing happens in our hearts or even our lives to contradict it, we just may go on for a long time. Very long.

My Change Point

I was in college and grappling with the rules at Grace College—check the paradox!

Now Grace is a wonderful school and I still recommend it. I had a good four years of college and four of seminary there.

Its name clearly defines its intention—to promote grace.

But we had plenty of rules back then, and I had even more for my own heart.

I was still trying to figure out how I could get enough points with God because that's just the subtle way I was raised.

No one went around saying it at our church; neither did my grandmother who was so into love and grace. But her additional rules for pleasing God were clear.

Like not shopping on Sundays.

Like giving ten percent of every dollar—no questions asked—to the church. When she gave us an allowance of a dollar, it was in change so we could tithe.

No one said we earn righteousness, but we surely worked hard at it.

I look back and smile and sum it up with a famous rule, "We don't smoke or chew or date the girls that do."

I shall never forget when this second of five verses hit me between the eyes and made me cry. It helped me finally feel secure in front of God's love. It is still at the top of my list.

> *But now a righteousness from God,*
> *apart from law, has been made known,*
> *to which the law and the prophets testify.*
> *This righteousness from God*
> *comes through faith in Jesus Christ*
> *to all who believe.*
> Romans 3:21

On the same day the verse hit me—I was sitting in the library—I also read about the gift of righteousness (Romans

5:17). And from that day on, with tears of joy, I accepted righteousness as a spiritual standing in front of God. A wonderful gift!

A direct gift from God made in response to my faith in His Son.

I have not doubted that part since.

Still, I hear it all the time: "Oh I believe those things, but I just don't think you can know for sure you have eternal life!"

Where did you get that? Where did you get that you can't know for sure?

I've never had anyone answer where they got it. They just believe it—you can't know for sure.

You can't really believe God.

I mean, most religious people are trying so hard to keep what they think are the things to do, and to get in with God.

"I've always felt that your good deeds are weighed against your bad deeds when you die, and that determines whether or not you go to heaven." An astute and well-educated man told me that.

Doing Our Best

"I try to do my best every day."

I've heard that sentence from parishioners, friends, strangers, and the scientist flying from Tucson to Chicago.

I didn't really want to talk to him. I wanted to take a nap.

He saw me reading my Bible at the start of the flight and asked if I were a pastor. Maybe he thought only the clergy read Bibles?

We got into a pretty heavy conversation about his spiritual emptiness. His words, not mine.

He had tried several churches. This man was one of the leading astronomers for the US government, and a graduate of the University of Chicago, no light place to study. He had accomplished a lot but felt like he was empty, and maybe flunking his spiritual life.

I thought it would be good to put everything on the table— or the fold-down tray at least on the back of the airplane seat. "If you died and went to heaven and God asked, 'Why should I let you in?' what would you say?"

It's a good question. It's not the way it's going to work, but it does put everything on the tray.

He thought a while, and went with what he thought would be his best answer: "I did my best."

That's what He would tell God to try to get in.

I was candid and I asked if he did do his best.

"No," was his answer, and it came with a grimace.

So I asked, "The first thing you say to God is going to be a lie?"

"I'm in trouble, aren't I?" He was sincere.

I then tried to explain the Romans 3 paragraph that changed my heart that day in the college library. It has settled into my soul and given me great consolation ever since.

The truth answers questions every human being asks if he is honest and willing to grapple with eternal issues.

RIGHTEOUSNESS IS A GIFT

But now a righteousness from God,
apart from law,
has been made known.
Romans 3:21

...and are justified [declared righteous]
freely by his grace
through the redemption that came
by Christ Jesus.
Romans 3:24

Righteousness Is Given.

You can say "righteousness" or even "spiritual perfection." Call it what you like, it is a recognition by God that your life is okay. That you are not carrying sin. That you are holy in His sight.

And it is a demand in the Bible that makes everybody close the book.

I was visiting in the home of someone who was facing the awful death of cancer. His family had not told him what the doctor said, but he probably assumed it was months or weeks away. His wife asked me to visit because she knew he liked the 60-second television spots I did about Christ and the church. He didn't like church, but he could handle the short spots.

When I went I could tell he was a little perturbed that she had sent for me. It was our first meeting.

We talked sports and cancer and then got even more serious about eternity.

It led to a declaration designed to get his attention: "You do know you have to be perfect to go to heaven?"

That ruffled him a little. I don't think he knew much theology, but he knew enough to say pretty strongly, "Well no one's perfect."

That's true.

He didn't know this, but he got that from the Bible. I guess he got it from his own experience too. Or maybe he knew me better than I thought.

Right, no one's perfect.

But you do have to be perfect to go to heaven. There are a lot of verses that command us to be perfect. One even says, "Without holiness, no one will see God."

So that means we're all in big trouble.

But what if "perfect" is a gift?

What if "perfect" is a state of the soul that God actually declares as true when we come to Him in a way that He wishes?

What if "perfect" is the way God sees us when the gift of the righteousness of His perfect Son covers us in His sight?

Romans 3 says it clearly.

> *But now, a righteousness from God, apart from law, has been made known.*
> *This righteousness from God comes through faith in Jesus Christ to all who believe.*
> Romans 3:23,24

Not **to** but **from**

Righteousness comes down from God. Romans 3:21 begins, "But now a righteousness from God...."

Religion might be described as our attempts to send righteousness up to God. Or to keep the law, the Ten Commandments. Which no one has ever done!

But this righteousness is from God.

Sinners Are in Trouble

Chapters before Romans 3:21 declare that everyone is guilty before a holy God. Most people would admit that; they just decide that it doesn't mean anything.

One prominent leader said, "I know I'm a sinner—but aren't we all?" He found relief with that; maybe there is power in numbers.

And he was right. But his inference was that it doesn't matter. Since we're all sinners, we're all in the same boat, and—here's their assumption—we're all going to make it.

Not true.

We have all fallen "short of the glory of God," which implies we're short of something that was a goal. Our goal was to get in with God or to be accepted by God. Instead we miss the mark.

Some more than others, indeed.

But we are guilty in front of a holy God and are not going to make it, as far as living with God. He can't accept sin.

Romans 1 and 2 have declared that we are all guilty because we go against creation—the signs of the design are everywhere!

And we go against our own consciences. Who has not broken his own rules? And the Bible defines that as sin.

The Remedy for All of Us

This verse that I discovered—I mean it was there and hit me right in the heart and right between the eyes one day—says that this "righteousness from God comes through faith in Jesus Christ, to all who believe" (Romans 3:22).

That means that God covers us with the righteousness or the perfection of Jesus Christ when we believe in Christ and trust Him. When we take Him at His word. When we rest our faith in Him.

It's hard to do because we would rather trust ourselves. We would rather decide that we're good enough to make it or we're doing so well that God's going to look at us and say, "Oh my, what a privilege to have you as my child."

Now I know I'm reeking with sarcasm here, and that no one goes around really saying it that way. That is, however, how we're acting when we try it on our own.

One of the kinder men in Akron joined me in a discussion one day at a leadership social. We got into serious issues—

I'm not sure how. But he told me about spiritual things and even church, "I'm just not into that kind of thing."

So to make him think, I wrote him a letter the next week. He was a leader of a bank.

I said in the letter that I wouldn't be paying our mortgage anymore. My explanation: "I'm not into that sort of thing anymore."

Surely he knew I was kidding, and we did pay our mortgage.

But everyone will get into this thing called spiritual life someday. I mean maybe even at the "final reckoning," as some used to call it.

Or maybe when they realize their cancer is pretty tough and they're not going to get over it.

Or maybe when they're in some other kind of ditch.

Everyone is into it. We don't get a choice.

And God is so into it that He offers something because He loves us. A gift.

The gift of righteousness and of forgiveness.

RIGHTEOUSNESS IS A GIFT NEEDED BY ALL SINNERS

For all have sinned
and fall short of the glory of God.
Romans 3:23

I'm trying to look at the context. Every Bible verse must be seen in its context.

You can rip anything out of the context and make nonsense out of it, or apply it any way you want.

Many people love the phrase, "God so loved the world." They bank on that to mean that they don't even have to respond to God in any way.

But the rest of the verse shows how He extended His love by giving Jesus Christ, and the end of the verse shows that we must believe in Christ to have eternal life.

That's the famous John 3:16 that a lot of people learned as little kids. But many like to stop at the first part; "God loves us."

One friend, a very successful leader in town, added to that, "God loves me, and my daddy said that God would never judge sin."

I remember asking kindly, "Where did your daddy get that?"

He didn't remember.

Could be his daddy got it from his daddy. Could be it was passed on from generation to generation, and no one knew the source.

Could be somebody way back made it all up – that God would never judge sin.

Maybe there was a daddy or a father there that never disciplined or punished his children, so he decided God never would either.

But the revelation of the Scriptures – I know I'm taking a lot of this from the Bible because I believe it's clearly true and clearly God's Word – says that a holy God can't just smile at sin and go, "Aw shucks."

What are sinners? They are people who fall "short" of the glory of God. They don't make it. They fall flat.

Who Falls Short

I have in my file written admissions from two very fine people that they needed a savior. That they are sinners who need help. One is Billy Graham and one was Mother Teresa.

Those two rank high on our "good people" lists! I have never talked with anyone who thought he was ahead of them in the good works column or the righteousness column.

Anyway, back to their written words, that they both need the Savior. They both refer to trusting Jesus Christ for their salvation.

There is no other way.

So if they fall short, I would have to say that I'm way behind. Maybe you would admit your own need.

Let's say we all decided to swim to England across the Atlantic Ocean, starting at Long Island.

Some of us swim decently. I might make it out a mile. You might make it five miles. Somebody else falls over in the waves near shore and drowns at a hundred yards.

And which of the people are dead?

The one who makes it five miles doesn't have any delight in making it farther than those who died close to shore.

And the one who seems better in contrast to others still falls way short of the target which is righteous perfection in front of a holy God.

We feel good about ourselves by comparison to others, not by lining up to the perfect condition or even the righteous demands of Christ.

The moral distance from God to us is gigantic, because of our sorry record and His holiness. How will we ever get to Him? It feels impossible.

Some people choose to ignore that distance or what God says about it in the Bible over and over again.

Romans 3:23 is clear. "All have sinned, and fall short of the glory of God." Very short. Way short. We make a mess of our spirits.

Maybe you're not as short as I am, of His glory; or I'm not as short as you are—but we're all short of His glory.

We people often say, "Well, at least I'm better than Charlie." And you're always better than someone you pick out who is worse than you are.

But the indictment abides. We are in trouble and cannot relate to God personally on our own.

But….

Christ to God for Us

God sent Jesus Christ into the world for the express purpose of dying on the cross for our sins. And the message of the Bible is that it is not enough to acknowledge that or salute as you drive by.

It is a personal trust and commitment.

It is based on what Christ did at the cross. The cross involved payment for sins. Judicial legal payment.

We should know what the cross did toward the holiness and laws of God.

What Christ did satisfied the holy laws of God. When He cried out, "My God, why have you forsaken me?" it was because all of our sins were on His back. There is no way we could ever take care of our own sins.

In the darkness of that moment He satisfied the holy laws of God and payment was made for our sins.

Romans 3:25 says, "God presented Christ as a sacrifice of atonement [satisfaction] through faith in his blood." "Atonement" means God's just laws are satisfied. The sin is paid for—by this substitute.

Can you believe that?

What in the world could I ever do about this by trying to earn my way? I fall short. Christ did it for us.

YOU DECIDE.

Now look at what God does toward people who believe. He justifies or declares righteous.

Romans 3:24 says, "We are justified freely by his grace... by Christ Jesus." Freely. Without cost to us!

He covers over our lives with the righteousness of Christ. Romans 5:17 calls this the gift of righteousness. He declares us perfect, " accepted in the beloved," covered by the righteousness of Christ. No wonder we can have confidence about eternal life if we really believe this.

A Gift Is a Gift

The gift of righteousness is about this grace—the word implies that we don't earn it on our own. It is totally a gift. It is nothing else but a gift.

No one can buy it or earn it.

Grace that is amazing is the act by which a holy God declares someone righteous.

Grace is the peculiar work of an entirely perfect God who decides He will cover us with the entirely perfect righteousness of His incarnate Son, Jesus the Christ. He will credit that righteousness of Christ to us. Read the clear verses.

That gets you past religion or the tension of trying to keep the Ten Commandments while hoping God doesn't notice when you break them.

This is totally the opposite of religion, which could be described as our way to attempt to climb to God, or earn an entrance to heaven.

There is more to this diagram of grace from this wonderful paragraph that changed my heart and practice.

Christ redeems or buys us and frees us. Here the arrow comes from Him to us. He has redeemed us by His own death, the Bible says.

Romans 3:24 says, "We are justified [declared righteous] freely by his grace through the redemption that came by Christ Jesus."

He sets us free, redeems us, from the sentence of the law over our lives.

In the days when the Romans letter was first read, slaves for sure knew the meaning of "redeem." It was when a slave was set free after being bought.

Trusting in God and His sacrifice on the cross means more than going to church or simply repeating some words.

It is actually trusting in who He is and what He did for you at the cross.

Our Response

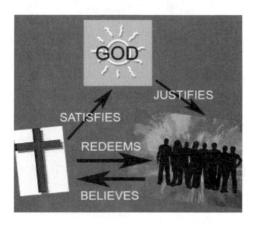

What must we do in our hearts?

RIGHTEOUSNESS IS A GIFT NEEDED BY ALL SINNERS AND RECEIVED BY FAITH

> *This righteousness from God*
> *comes through faith in Jesus Christ*
> *to all who believe.*
> Romans 3:22

We believe in Christ and in what He did out of pure generosity.

This Romans 3 paragraph refers to those who have "faith in his blood" (3:24) or "who have faith in Jesus" (3:26).

Faith means "belief." It is the noun. "Believe" is the verb. It means to rest in or commit to.

I often talk to people who say, "I believe, but I just don't think anybody can know for sure you have eternal life or are a follower of Christ."

"Well, what it is that you believe?" I always ask.

"Well, I believe Christ died for our sins and all that, but I just don't think anybody can know for sure…"

The point is, do we believe or not? Do we actually trust, have faith, that God sent His Son not only to die on the cross and rise again, but that it would really work?

It did.

He did.

He is the Savior!

He shares the glory of His righteousness and forgives us.

That is the glorious Good News, as long as we are willing to believe.

This wave of truth washed over me in thirty minutes of private worship in a library of Grace College as I studied Romans 3 for a class.

And embraced it for my confidence.

So as I sputter inside and seek God's strength for the day, this is total joy. Access has been given. And received.

Can you believe this?

If God declared red is blue, it is blue; go along with it. He will eventually prove it to be right. But actually everything God does will turn out to be sensible and true, not contradictory to facts.

If He says that when Jesus died all our sins were placed on Him, we should accept that. We should not waste a moment of sleep by worrying about whether or not our sins are forgiven.

Grace Through Jesus

So grace is the act by which God does for us what we could never do for ourselves, and He does it in the person of the one He calls "his beloved son," in whom He is well pleased.

He is the one who said, "I am the bread of life. He who comes to me will never go hungry, and he who believes in me will never be thirsty" (John 6:35).

Not long after that He said, "'If anyone is thirsty, let him come to me and drink. Whoever believes in me, as the scripture has said, streams of living water will flow from within him.' By this he meant the Spirit, whom those who believed in him were later to receive" (John 7:38,39).

That's where I got the idea that if we really believe in Jesus Christ we don't have to add mixed drinks of religion and our good works on top of that to become His children.

That's where I got that it's believing in a person, including the work that He did on the cross.

That's what the apostle Paul, one of the chief architects of theology—he wrote by inspiration – that's what he said when he defined the gospel in 1 Corinthians 15:1-4. It wasn't about feelings or trying to do good. It was about our faith and the death and resurrection (on the third day) of Jesus the Christ.

How can we miss this? God did it for us! Our record is sorry. His gift is His Son.

These Other Ideas

Where did we get this idea that each of us must be sincere and work up our own religious sweat to get to Heaven—holy sweat equity is the common view of people!

We got it on the street.

We got it the same place that I got the facts of life from a friend in sixth grade, and he was all wrong. (And I still wonder how he did in marriage!)

Some misrepresent these facts by saying they believe in Jesus Christ, but then they have very little consistency in their love and grace. They look untouched by God.

It's really disheartening.

We all fail at times, but there are some who claim the name of Christ and then practice indiscretion and prejudice.

There are people who say these things and then look like all they do is follow their own selfish desires in life.

So I apologize for them.

You should ask them just as I should, "Where did you get that—this idea that you can believe in Jesus and then live any way that you want?"

One of my favorite people in all the world is the man who managed the building of the Sears tower in Chicago. He retired soon after that, and I get to see him almost every summer on vacation times near Lake Michigan.

He's a great thinker. A graduate of Notre Dame, he likes to ponder theology.

One time after I was done trying to explain this way of righteousness, and the diagram you have just seen, he put it succinctly when he asked it this way: "You're trying to tell me that a man two thousand years ago did something on a cross that made expiation for all my sins!"

And I said that was true. Then I realized how hard it is to believe that – that one person, that long ago, did something that potentially could free every person in the whole wide world.

I know it's hard to believe.

But is it easier to believe that God doesn't really care about sin?

Is it easier to believe that we people whom we know pretty well could somehow fool our holy God and make Him think that we're actually very, very nice and very, very right?

Is it easier to believe that all the religions of the world are right when they contradict each other on many points, especially about how we go to heaven?

The Fine Was Paid

I once heard Billy Graham tell the story of being caught for speeding in a small town in Georgia, a "speed trap," as he called it.

It was one of those places where you walk into the justice of the peace, receive the fine, pay the bill, and get on your way.

My brother told me about them.

In this case the justice of the peace, the judge, recognized Billy Graham and thanked him for what he is doing in America. But he added, "I must give you the fine."

As he gave that to Billy Graham he also reached into his own pocket for his checkbook. Graham said that in a moment he received the fine in one hand and the check for the amount of the fine, payable to the court, in the other hand.

He gave them both back to the judge and drove away carefully.

What a great illustration for our lives and our attitudes toward God and His call for holiness. His just demands abide, but He pays the fine for us.

There is a way.

You decide.

III

There Is No Secret

I was on a flight from the West Coast seated beside a person who could have been a college football tackle. He had been up all night drinking at a party, and now he was sleeping it off.

I was in the aisle seat and a delightful lady, a medical doctor from Cleveland, was over by the window.

I think we both wished the big lug would have chosen the window. The few times the doctor had to get out, she had to crawl over him. He never woke up.

Our conversation around him was about her work and her involvement in the science of medicine.

Later as we were reading she saw that I was checking the Bible. I was going to be teaching for about two hours the next week at a Hebrew college in Cleveland on "the Christian view of the Messiah." Probably one of my most serious assignments ever.

I was reading from Isaiah 53.

"What are you reading?" she asked.

"It's Isaiah 53, and it seems so obvious that it's about a person," I responded. "Do you know the chapter?"

She did not.

I said it was about the Messiah who was "pierced for our transgressions...crushed for our iniquities" (Isaiah 53:5).

I added a verse famous for Jews and Christians alike: "We all, like sheep, have gone astray, each of us has turned to his own way; and the Lord has laid on him the iniquity of us all" (53:6).

I asked if she knew what that meant. She showed that she didn't care what it meant when she said, "To me, whatever you believe is truth for you." It was to end the discussion.

Instead I asked her if she practiced that in medicine.

"Of course not," she said pretty quickly.

I went further, testing her patience, but feeling like it was worth the thought: "Do you hope the pilot flies like that? That whatever seems true is the way he flies?"

"Of course not."

But to her and to many that I have met in my adult years, the truth of theology is pretty subjective. No longer is theology "the queen of the sciences." It's rather the choice of the masses. It is as variable as fashion.

We simply need to believe something.

We don't say the same thing when we talk about math or spelling. If you don't follow the rules in math, your results are wrong.

A misspelled word isn't correct because you say so.

The Christian Life

Personal faith in Jesus brings His forgiveness and righteousness.

And then the Christian life starts.

But sometimes the obedience part seems very hard, especially if we just choose to believe what seems true for us, or if we grit our teeth and try to do what's right.

It just does not work that way.

So What Is Next?

People register faith with God and say they believe in Jesus Christ. Sometimes, they even understand the gift of righteousness and forgiveness, the two parts of what is called salvation.

And then they get on with conventional independent living.

Often because the path of Jesus just plain seems too hard.

There are these commands in the Bible to serve others—the picture of Jesus washing feet is daunting.

And the call to love your enemies, let alone forgive everyone and never get even, is intimidating.

Too much.

So most people give up.

They let a little sin in their heart and it doesn't feel so bad. Nothing gets black and blue on their chest or lies don't show on their forehead, and it's easy to just drift through life. Many who say they follow Christ think about it very little.

Even when some of these people hear about things like the fact that Jesus will walk with us, it's hard to figure out what this all means.

Does He make our decisions for us?

I mean, all of us decided what we would eat today and what clothes we would wear. Even where we would go.

So what does it mean to live with the Lord in your heart and in your life?

Often kids take it pretty seriously when they're little and then they hit the teen years and hormones kick in, and they are out of here.

We err either on the side of dropping out or working so hard to try to please Christ that we really get tired. I mean really tired.

And people who get tired also drop out in the end.

My Change Point

That's where I was. Doing seminary and studying theology and even getting good grades, I still found I was dutifully obeying.

And I can do duty as well as the next guy.

Somewhere I was taught to finish your day and to play the game hard and to hustle in the fourth quarter.

So I can do that with my spirit and my religion too.

But I read Galatians 2:20, and my heart was changed, not on the first reading but after careful study. In fact, I made this the subject of my Master's thesis in seminary because I really wanted to understand it. The verse goes like this.

> *I have been crucified with Christ*
> *and I no longer live,*
> *but Christ lives in me.*
> *The life I live in the body,*
> *I live by faith in the Son of God,*
> *who loved me and gave himself for me.*
> Galatians 2:20

Any questions?

Many of them.

The thesis I wrote was many pages long, and I doubt that many people have read it.

But I got it. I love it. And I hope I can express it to you.

It's Paul the Apostle talking about his life related to the Law—the big Law, the Ten Commandments and the hold they have on us from a holy God. The verse is also talking about how to live the daily Christian life.

It goes like this.

WE DIED WHEN CHRIST DID

*I have been crucified with Christ
and I no longer live.*
Galatians 2:20

That's what God says. We don't have to feel it or understand it totally. But we should try to figure out what it
means.

It means that when we put our faith in Jesus Christ, God
counts it as true that when Jesus died we did too.

We started over.

True, this is not effective until we place our faith in Christ
– see chapter 2. But it means that when we put our faith in
Christ and trust Him as Savior and Lord, God counts that as
starting over. We died and started again.

We started a new life – in His sight and, He hopes, soon
in ours.

Can you believe it?

YOU DECIDE.

Marriage as an Illustration

If you are married, when you got married you started over.
You died to your single life.

When I got married the single Knute Larson quit.
Expired. Stopped.

And that's the way I aimed to live from then on.

It is truth we have to accept, though we can contradict
it and live as if it's not true. Paul is saying what is meant to
be true in each of our lives—that when we place our faith in
Christ we stop living as a "single" person and begin to live in
combination with Jesus Christ.

So don't be shocked by Paul's metaphor that we died. Don't pretend you're no longer there. Don't act as if this is so mysterious you can't take it, so you have to go on to the next page, which just could be Ephesians in your Bible. It follows Galatians.

Ephesians is all about living "in Christ," a phrase repeatedly emphasized.

And that's what we're talking about here – we stop living in Larson and start living in Christ.

You put your name in that sentence.

The single-you dies and you begin to live in combination.

Too many people simply see the commands for Christians in the New Testament or anywhere in the Bible and they decide they can't do it.

Where did you get that?

They got it from experience. They got it from trying to love that naughty, selfish narcissistic man at work, and they can't do it. So they just shelve the idea.

Look at it another way.

WE DIED WHEN CHRIST DID, YET STILL LIVE IN COMBINATION

And I no longer live,
but Christ lives in me.
Galatians 2:20

Paul explains how that works: "The life I live in the body, I live by faith in the Son of God, who loved me and gave himself for me" (2:20).

Paul still lives, but not the way he used to. Now he lives in combination.

Christ lives in him and in us – all of us who believe and trust Christ as Savior.

As with marriage, our single life died when we married.

As with marriage, we live in combination. Together. As one. In a mysterious connection.

With Christ, we have found a spiritual marriage united in love.

So we are meant to be dead to ourselves, dead to the former life, unresponsive to our life without Christ. But "married" to Christ spiritually, intent on living in combination.

Living by faith in Christ and by believing what He says and what He has instructed us to do. We live in His power to help us.

That's the combination life.

So there is no secret about how to live the Christian life.

There should be no excuses like, "That's an impossible way to live!"

Where did you get that?

People got that by trying to live not in combination but in personal religious hustle and hard work. Keep the rules! Go to church! Do what is right!

Even after believing Christ died for our sins we can believe that we've got to make the rest of it work ourselves. It's tiring.

The Combination Explained

Paul has experienced what it means for Christ to live in him. It's an experience of living in combination, of trusting Christ and seeking to walk with His strength but also with faith in Him on a daily basis.

So many get spooked by talk about the Holy Spirit, especially when the preacher on TV pronounces it, the Ho-oh-ly Spirit, or the Holy Ghost!

The Spirit is simply Christ in us when we start over by faith.

It is such a crucial issue in the Bible, that we died to self. We are asked to believe that what God has said is already true—that we started life over. That our "single life" died when we put our faith in Christ and He came into our lives.

So Paul is saying that the "old Paul" died when he met Christ. He no longer lives that old way.

Now he lives in combination with Christ in his personal life.

Sometimes in the Bible that "single" life is called the "old nature."

Ephesians 4:22 tells us to move away from that "old nature," and live a new way.

You can go crazy trying to figure out which part of you died! Is it the ego or the inner instincts?

It's the old me. The old you. The you without Christ. It's that simple and it's that hard.

It's hard to live in combination. It's simple to understand that we should.

Back to marriage—it's hard to live in combination.

Can you be married and still live as if you're single? I often ask that question in a small audience and people have to think. They know you shouldn't live that old way, but they know it's easy to drift back.

I forgot to tell my wife one time that a bunch of people were coming for dinner. I was living like a single. I was forgetting to communicate.

All of us forget to share things. Especially men.

It's easy to make a decision without taking your husband or wife into consideration.

It's easy to make a decision in life without realizing what Christ would think or what the Scriptures say or where His strength can come in.

So the life in combination is the life that is authentic as a Christian.

The Other Ways

People make up all sorts of ways to gain strength in their Christian life. To follow Christ. I've heard it 100 times—"I feel better when I go to church on Sunday."

"It changes the rest of the week for me."

Where did they get that?

YOU DECIDE.

The "secret" of the Christian life is not in rules but living in combination with Christ, honoring His Spirit in combination with our spirit.

Maturing in our faith means growing in grace and in the Word of God. It is simply resting in the finished work of Christ while seeking to please Him by the way we live.

The Bible tells us to put off the old nature, but it also tells us to put on the new nature—that's Christ in you, in combination.

WE DIED WHEN CHRIST DID YET STILL LIVE IN COMBINATION, AND ALL THIS IS BY FAITH

The life I live in the body,
I live by faith in the Son of God,

who loved me
and gave himself for me.
Galatians 2:20

Faith means believing. And believing always means accepting as truth the content that God has given.

"Faith comes by hearing, and hearing by the Word of God" (Romans 10:9).

This is to be done by faith. By believing. By taking the content of Scripture and believing it is true and then doing it.

It's that simple.

People often have the impression that it means that you always feel good about Scripture or what God has said.

That's just a rumor we picked up.

Everybody knows that love is action, not just feelings. Good marriages keep growing and getting stronger all the time not because people feel like it all the time, but because they do what is right.

The covenant that they made at the wedding produces the actions of love and the actions produce the feelings of love.

And the feelings keep growing because the actions keep coming.

Stop the actions because you no longer honor your covenant, and the feelings are going to die.

People say it all the time: "We don't love each other anymore."

I've heard it 100 times and so have you.

Well maybe I've heard it more because I have pastored all this time. But people use it as an excuse, and really believe love has disappeared!

But the reason they do not feel love is that they have stopped the actions of love. Couples stop being kind, listening, and taking walks—the actions that produced the love feelings in the first place.

They didn't fall in love, but they grew in actions of love because they were willing to commit to each other. And then at the wedding they really made the grand commitment.

The same thing can be said about our relationship with Christ. We can't live a life of faith with our feelings. Today, I feel good about Christ. Tomorrow, I'm ambivalent. On Sunday, I'll crank up the emotions again.

No, I should live in combination and obey Him and live by faith with the commitment I have made.

That means believing that Christ is right and true and therefore doing what He has said.

In this way, we grow in our faith.

We make ourselves do what's right because we believe it is true.

That's what it means to live by faith, trusting that Jesus Christ is really the Son of God and really true.

If He Is

If you were walking down the street with a person who said He is the Son of God, you would do everything He said. If He told you to act, you would not say, "I don't feel like it."

Not if you really believed He is the Son of God.

Faith means we believe He is the Son of God and therefore we believe He is telling us what is best. He is bright. He is right. He is light.

And we're willing to obey.

So when I understood Galatians 2:20 I understood what is not a secret, but what is the central core of the Christian life—to live in combination with Jesus Christ.

It changed my heart to seek His strength and His truth, to live in combination.

Learning to Know Him

Americans tend to be independent. We are proud to go it alone.

Instead the Christian life is meant to be a life lived in combination—you and the Lord whom you love.

To do so, we have to study Christ.

There is this famous verse in Hebrews 12:1 and 2 that tells us to be looking to Jesus Christ as we live this life. Then we "will not grow weary and lose heart," as it says.

And that means we've got to look at Him not with some subjective experience of seeing His shadow on the wall or seeing His picture on a taco, but rather by looking in the Gospels. Watch how He lives. Study His ways.

Pray to Him and ask for His strength, indeed, but make sure you get some content about how He wants us to live.

How else could we live in combination, if we did not know some of the things He did.

How did He relate to losers? How did He love sinners? What did He do?

One Way It Worked

One of the small ways I have experienced His presence and strength has been in attempts to create racial unity.

When I was little, a few in our small fundamentalist church made jokes about people of color. As I recall, sometimes right after a sermon on love!

My dad grew up in Iowa and would sometimes use racial slurs. Even as a teenager I knew it was wrong and I corrected him.

And as I pastored I realized that some of these prejudices or just plain mean ideas existed in the church. The church of Jesus Christ. The church of faith. The church of love.

When I moved to Akron in 1983, this holy discontent inside me came up more and more.

Early in my tenure, I invited Pastor Ronald Fowler, the dean of pastors in Akron, into my life. We sat at lunch and I asked a favor. Could he help me in this area of racial understanding, reconciliation, and unity?

That friendship, which sputtered briefly at first, became one of the most important ingredients in my life. Twenty-three years of meeting together and laughing together and helping each other with love have made this one of the strongest bonds in my heart.

After a few years we got our churches doing a few things together. Friendships formed with people of both places. A number of other churches of predominately African-American and predominately white joined together to form similar partnerships.

We called ours "Allies," partners in the war against racial prejudice.

Annual events and some ministry projects to others brought combination strength. And love.

We expanded it with the help of a pastor with a Pentecostal background, and started "Love Akron," a gathering to bridge these gaps and also theological ones as leaders of churches and ministries in the city would meet together to pray.

That remains strong. It unites. It relaxes.

Love grows.

Out of that combination ministry arose "Imagine Unity," a venture of that organization and about five others, including some that are predominately black churches, to work together and pray together and do some things that help promote true unity. We signed together a "Pledge of Unity," a personal pledge of allegiance to speak well of each other and to grow in understanding and love.

It's a long journey, and you never quite reach it. But it is a good journey.

It's something you do in combination with Christ, because of His love.

It is the way He would like to do it with us.

So...

I still get mixed up. I still try to impress God.

I walk across a parking lot and pick up a piece of trash and think God might be impressed with my servant's spirit.

But when my heart is clean, and as I start the day, I realize that my focus is meant to be on love for Christ. I must seek to live by what I believe, which is what it means to live by faith. And then I know that it won't be just me living, but Christ living in me. This would be a combination style. A marriage with Christ and His Spirit. It takes away all the pressure of trying to perform or to look good to God. "Religion" gives way to a relationship of love.

I like it very much. I hope you do.

YOU DECIDE.

IV

We Are Not Under the Law

Ok, I admit it. I'm a recovering people-pleaser and legalist. I should be in a support group where you start by saying, "My name is Knute Larson, and I am a prisoner."

I was taught by a few people to care way too much about what others think and to worry an extreme amount about what God thinks, even in issues where we have freedom to choose.

Now hang on for the whole ride through this chapter, because there is no freedom intended by God for people to do whatever they want with their bodies or their lives. But there is a wonderful freedom for everyone who is willing to follow the truth.

The truth sets us free.

But I'm getting ahead of myself. My own bondage came from the same kind of religion that hits so many conservative Protestants and conscientious Catholics and even members of other faiths. We were so rigid that certain things are right and wrong, and that it would not be good if God saw you do some of those things.

As a child I sang:

Oh be careful little hands what you do.
Oh be careful little hands what you do.
For the Father up above, is looking down in love.
Oh be careful little hands what you do.

The song went on in a similar fashion to the ears, eyes, feet, and mind. I had to be careful about hearing, seeing, going, or thinking.

Indeed, we should be careful, but I'm not sure whether the Father was looking down in love or looking to find fault!

One Sunday school teacher who didn't like movies warned us that if we were in a theatre when Jesus came back to the earth as promised, we would not go with Him on His return back to heaven! I remember being scared to death coming out of "King Kong" with my dad, brother, and sister. I was sure there would be car wrecks because of the return of Christ and the launching into space of some of the drivers who were believers.

And I would be left behind.

I got over that one gradually, and I still see a movie or two every year.

But it's hard to believe, when you're brought up religiously, as they say, that there is a freedom for choices in areas where God is not clear.

Coming to Akron

The biggest grappling I had with this issue of choice was 26 years ago when considering coming to Akron, Ohio, to pastor The Chapel.

I was a pastor in Ashland, Ohio, about 45 minutes away, with a wonderful 15 years under my belt and in my heart. The church had grown from 231 on the first day to about one thousand more than that often, and I loved the people like everything. So did my wife.

When The Chapel sent me a postcard to see if I would like to talk with them, I shifted into people-pleasing mode and wondered if I should even consider this.

I did, with hesitation, and it got to be fairly serious.

The long process took over a year because the church in Akron had made their own policy that the 18 people leading this had to be unanimous, and I was stalled at 17-1 on step five of nine major steps.

Word got out that I was considering this change.

A very good friend and member of our main board in Ashland, but also an occasional water-skiing friend: "How could you do this to us?" he asked.

I had no answer.

One lady put her feelings on the table: "Is this your climb up the corporate ladder?" I guess that's because The Chapel was much bigger.

I lost 19 pounds while considering this, because I was worrying about what others were thinking. It felt like divorce. I had already been through that with my parents, and I knew how awful it was. It couldn't be right.

I wrote down ten "doors" that had to open if we were to come—I don't think I'll ever do anything but protest if I hear anyone else doing that. One was that our two daughters would be willing to move to Akron—they told us at first that if we left Ashland they would stay! Another was related to the bank renewing our construction loan in Ashland—they said they wouldn't if I would leave because I was the "key man."

Other doors were related to some national issues related to the fellowship of churches I was in.

I wasn't in any kind of freedom here—I was in a bondage that I built for myself and that others helped me to build.

The Chapel by practice was just a little different in a couple of areas from the distinctives of the church I had pastored for 15 years, so I had to figure out if those were traditions or if I would be disobeying the Lord by leaving them.

My study made me realize the differences were in a third circle of importance. Christ and the Word of God as inspired are in the middle of the circle, along with the need for conversion by faith and trust.

The secondary circle probably includes issues where we're pretty firm, including the need for baptism and the need for church involvement and missions and things like that.

The third circle includes areas where many Christians differ. There you simply have to have freedom to choose your own conviction and not judge other people for their choices!

But many times we put ourselves in a stance that we think everything is primary and inflexible.

So on the day that I had to tell The Chapel whether or not I would come to "candidate," as they used to call it, I was still feeling the bondage of hurting people's feelings. I was not free to make choices that would either grieve a church or move me in areas that are not clearcut in the Bible.

I had not yet gained any of the 19 pounds back, and I still was not my happy self.

My Change Point

I read the book of Galatians in the Bible the day I had to make the phone call to get in or get out. I read the whole book. It's a great letter (nice of me to say so).

But I got stuck on this one: "It is for freedom that Christ has set us free. Stand firm then and do not let yourselves be burdened again by a yoke of slavery" (Galatians 5:1).

I read it again and again. I knew the context—about law and how we want to please God.

Before this faith came, we were held prisoners by the law, locked up until faith should be revealed. So the law was put in charge to lead us to Christ that we

might be justified by faith.
Now that faith has come, we are no longer under the
supervision of the law.
Galatians 3:23–25

That day I applied these verses to my decision to take another step with The Chapel.

The verse hit me between the eyes, but also in the middle of my heart.

I made the phone call.

Actually my wife did not know for sure what I was going to say when I left our rented cottage in Michigan to go to the phone. No cell phones in those days, and no phone in the little cottage we rented for 15 years. And I was still scared.

I drove to a pay phone alongside the Red Arrow Highway, still one of my favorite roads in the whole world. I said yes.

Yes we would begin a new adventure. Yes we would candidate, not knowing if there would be a freedom to come, but knowing there was a freedom in my heart.

Yes I could disappoint some people who loved me. Yes I was free to make personal decisions such as this.

And the verse is for all of us.

CHRIST SET US FREE

It is for freedom
that Christ has set us free.
Stand firm, then,
and do not let yourselves be burdened again
by a yoke of slavery.
Galatians 5:1

We are not under the bondage of the law. If you break the law, you're going to die by the law. You break the law, and you are under the penalty of the law.

Separation from God.

But we are not slaves to the law. When Jesus Christ came He fulfilled the law perfectly, every jot and tittle, as they used to say in His day. And when He died He paid the curse of my breaking the law. Yours too.

So when I trust Him—this is the message of Galatians— His keeping the law counts for me and His penalty for the law counts for me.

From the first part of that I get Christ's righteousness credited to my "account," my spiritual status in front of this holy God. From the second part I can know that the penalty of sin was totally paid for me.

This is huge.

The Children of God

Paul tells the Galatians and us, "You are all sons of God through faith in Christ Jesus" (Galatians 3:26).

He even says that if you "belong to Christ, then you are Abraham's seed, and heirs according to the promise" (3:29).

That means I am a spiritual Jew, in the line of the promises with all physical Jews, and it means also that I receive the great blessing of the Messiah who is in the line of Abraham and David, and who brings the kingdom into my heart.

Paul tells the people in Galatians 3:4: "When we were children, we were in slavery under the basic principles of the world. But when the time had fully come, God sent his son, born of a woman [interesting choice of words if you believe the virgin birth], born under law, to redeem those under law, that we might receive the full rights of sons" (4:3-5).

We are children of God, no longer slaves, but his sons and daughters. Heirs of the kingdom, as this letter puts it. And free indeed!

Free to avoid worrying about whether we're allowed to make choices in God's will. Free in Christ from the horrible bondage of just trying to be religious. Free from trying to please people.

And we all know what that means. It means trying to keep rules and trying to look good and trying to please the pastor or the rabbi or the father or the neighbor or even the parents.

It's just not the way in which we find the joys of following Christ.

The Freedom of Grace

I remember when my dad and I were engaged in one of our most serious discussions ever. He was 46 and felt he had lived "outside the will of God" all his life—at least from age 21 on.

The reason: his Swedish Baptist Church in Iowa and his very Swedish Baptist parents told him that because he didn't go into the ministry, he was missing God's best for his life.

He and my mother, his new sweetheart, quit their Christian college to get married.

They moved to Harrisburg, Pennsylvania, and he started life over as a railroad worker and later a used car salesman.

But from age 21 to 46, he thought he was God's second string. Living and experiencing God's love, but outside the circle of His will. Whatever that means.

It's an old wives' tale, that's what it is. It's an urban legend.

I mean check in the Bible to see what God said about David, the adulterer and murderer, after David repented. By His own description God had His writers call David "a man after His own heart."

It was because God had given David freedom from the past. Freedom from his guilt, and a new standing.

Surely God wants every one of us to live in that freedom.

Some people even write about "secondary virginity"! The idea is the fact that we can start over with God. His middle name is mercy. His constant joy is forgiveness.

He wants us to be free from our own guilt and from blaming ourselves.

So many believe on paper that God has forgiven them when they have asked such a favor, but they just cannot forgive themselves. Or their husbands. Or their wives.

Come on!

You decide.

My dad cried and realized as we looked at the descriptions of King David that you can come back to please God, who does not keep bringing up the past. Our mistakes are not on a list God keeps.

From that day, my dad began to walk his journey of life with the Lord's presence in mind.

With freedom.

CHRIST SET US FREE TO LIVE IN FREEDOM

It is for freedom
that Christ has set us free.
Galatians 5:1

And that means we can choose our way. We do not have to put what people think ahead of what we desire.

When Martin Luther made his famous statement, "Love God and do as you please," he was not calling for promiscuous sex or ridiculous rebellion. He was simply saying that when we really love God (and we keep His commandments because we love Him), in areas where God has not spoken – like whether or not I should take the position in Akron!—we have freedom to choose what we think is best.

We can decide what movies to watch, whether to have wine with dinner, what to wear. In all these areas and thousands more, we are free to choose.

I even know people who felt like God had a direct opinion about what college they should go to, and therefore they did not feel free to choose a college based on their tests and their opinions, but would seek some kind of a sign from God about where they should go to school.

Something like my ten "doors."

What if God just wants us to choose those things, using careful discretion and fine wisdom and even the counsel of other people?

Maybe not the counsel of the one who said, "You just can't do this to us!"

When people talk about the will of God, they often mean what many of us were taught when we were little, that God has an opinion about just about everything, and that we should seek to find out what He wants us to do. Certainly about college or marriage or big decisions.

I bet you've heard this if you grew up in church: "I'm asking the Lord what He would have me to do." It was always interesting to me that it's not "what the Lord wants me to do," but what He "would have me do."

There is just something religious about that way of saying it.

Sort of like when we prayed for people who were traveling, that they would have "journey's mercies." I always wanted to just pray that they would not wreck.

Sovereign Will

But back to the "will of God"—a phrase used many times in the Bible. But it's something like this: there is the sovereign will of God—and all we can do here is trust Him.

That means that He works "all things after the counsel of His own will" (Ephesians 1:11).

It means that He's going to end the world at the exact time He wishes and that He's going to make things happen the way He wishes. And we cannot figure it out. We can pray about things and launch all the faith toward God that we can, but we can't figure out what He's thinking all the time. No way.

I doubt that He tells people directly what college to attend.

Maybe He just cares how you live in the dorm and how you do your studies.

The sovereign will of God is the trust we have that He, as Isaiah said, sits enthroned above the circle of the earth, and rules and reigns and will be glorified by the entire world someday. No question.

And all we can do is trust.

No one can be free of this sovereign will of God.

It is what it is.

Moral Will

But there is a second use of "the will of God" in the Bible, and that's about His moral will. That's what we know as right or wrong in the Bible.

When Paul prayed that the people at Colossae would be "filled with the knowledge of His will with all spiritual wisdom and understanding" (Colossians 1:14), that was the will of God that Paul was talking about. The revealed will. What God says in the Scriptures.

In one sense we already know what that is – we just read it. Don't lie. Don't steal. Don't commit adultery. Don't do things that destroy the unity of your church family or your own.

Forgive your enemies plus the people that are mean to you. Make an honest living and take care of your family.

Don't be jealous of others.

There are many such clear directions from God. These are His will. His moral will.

And here all we can do is obey.

Well, we can disobey, but should not.

God's moral will is what gives our freedom its limits. They always used to say that my freedom ends where your nose begins. That makes sense.

But freedom also ends where the truth of the Scripture begins. Either we have a God who cares how we live or we don't, of course. And freedom is related to truth. In fact, according to Jesus, "The truth shall make you free" (John 8:32).

But free to obey. Free from our old slavery of selfishness, prejudices, and guilt.

Free to do what's right, to love others.

Free to obey the greatest command of all—"to love God with all our hearts and souls and minds and strength; and then to love our neighbor as our self" (Matthew 22:37–39).

That's true freedom.

That may be the exact freedom people wish for when they take on extra rules of religion or their church.

In connecting with Christ by faith, we are set free from guilt and even the power of sin, which tugs at our hearts to pull us down. But He shows His freedom to be present only when we obey this moral will. We are free to choose but not free to avoid the consequences.

Shepherding Will

Let's call the third area of God's will His "shepherding will." And here all we can do is to seek wisdom.

Wisdom to make good choices.

Jeanine and I were free to come to Akron—we just didn't know it at first.

You are free to be a carpenter or to be a barber or to be a teacher or to be a pastor. You must decide.

When you look back, as I do, you will see God's shepherding in your life. He really provided needs and brought people into your life and did some things that helped you make a good choice. But He never whispered those choices or gave them out loud.

Some people have said to me, "God told me to tell you this." That could put me in bondage, since I'd better do it if God told them to tell me to do it!

Or I can be free just to treat that as a very strong opinion this person has.

I even knew a guy in college who told a girl that God had told him that he should marry her.

That didn't change her mind about not doing it. As I recall she said that if God told her the same thing, she would go ahead.

In my mind, that was just a very strong urge that guy had, and he gave credit to God.

In this area of shepherding decisions, we pray for wisdom and then make choices. The Bible tells us we will be responsible for our choices, and that God will give us wisdom.

But we have to accept the freedom to make the choices and then live with them, without waiting for a voice.

Not Easy for Me

I guess I still take polls in my heart at times. I wonder what people will think and I act accordingly. To win their favor.

And there's nothing wrong with trying to please people.

But not when it comes to a general way of life. We are free to do what is right, free to make our choices, free to seek God's wisdom and go by it.

And that is a freedom indeed!

The truth is, we only have one to please.

I remember the story about one of the most famous of the chiefs of staff in the White House—John Sununu, who had been labeled a lion, a tough guy.

One of the reporters—this was written up in *Time* magazine—had asked him about his difficult job. The way he put it was, "Isn't your job very hard?"

And John Sununu replied, "Not at all."

Then this former Governor of New Hampshire explained, "It's not hard because I only have one constituent."

One person to please.

Let us live that way more and more. With one constituent. One Lord. One person to please.

That is freedom.

CHRIST SET US FREE TO LIVE IN FREEDOM, NOT IN THE BURDEN OF SLAVERY

Stand firm, then,
and do not let yourselves
be burdened again
by a yoke of slavery.
Galatians 5:1

It is indeed slavery to live in sin, or under the demands of the Ten Commandments. We cannot break the bondage ourselves. No way.

Ask anyone who has "quit smoking any time he wishes." Twelve times in total!

Or the most of us who have decided never to gossip again. And then again.

We just cannot shake our sins by ourselves.

Let us admit it.

And the call here is to live in the freedom that comes with the truth of Jesus.

I simply am calling you to the free joy of our Lord.

But it comes only with truth and the person who said so bluntly, "I am the…truth" (John 14:6).

Am I ever glad I came to Akron!
Am I ever glad for freedom!

YOU DECIDE.

V

One Thing More

I was crying. The song we were singing was one I can sing in my sleep—"Amazing Grace."

We were standing in the front row of our church sanctuary. I would be going up to the pulpit to preach right after "When we've been there ten thousand years."

No one had said much before the song, which was concluding 25 minutes of hymns and choir and Scripture, prayer, and offering. It's just that 26 years of amazing grace indeed flashed through my emotions.

I even remembered the eternal spiritual connection with the Lord I had accepted by faith when young, and the strength to lead I got as a timid child and teenager.

"Through many dangers, toils, and snares, I have already come."

I thanked God for the difficult start at The Chapel in 1983. The revered beloved pastor of 23 years, also the son of the founding pastor, had left a year before to serve another church, and a few hundred of the over three thousand took their disappointments out on me.

But peace and church unity and grace quickly won the day, and I was thankful as I remembered.

Many came to faith. Many came to church.

We went from two to five worship services on Sunday, gradually, one at a time.

We expanded local and global missions and service projects with joy, and the "school spirit" was like a bonfire before the big football game.

We started helping other churches, expanded our Adult Bible Fellowships—our version of adult Sunday school—and started minute spots on radio and TV.

God helped us to begin three branch churches and then take the huge leap of "one church in two locations," the second campus being nine miles down the highway, in Green.

And 2500 people came to that second campus the first day we started.

Many came to faith. Many embraced the grace of God for the first time forever.

My memory made it through all that by the time we sang, "We've no less days to sing God's praise..."

And I was just grateful. Just plain thankful.

None of these gifts is deserved.

They were all given.

That is the nature of a gift. You can't buy a gift. It comes without strings.

I was crying because I am grateful.

My Change Point

This hit me especially hard and in the middle of my heart at the time I was getting ready to announce a transition to teaching and coaching young pastors and slowing down to grandfather better.

I was reading in my book-filled study next to a nice office for meetings with people. As I read this verse for the hundredth time it shook my heart. I embraced it.

For who makes you different
from anyone else?
What do you have that you did not receive?
And if you did receive it, why do you boast
as though you did not?
I Corinthians 4:7

The question is clear. No answer is needed. We should not be proud.

I certainly know every good personal life-change or positive move or growth at The Chapel was a kind favor from God. A gift.

Shall I be grateful?

It's not that God is simply trying to wipe out pride. Pride won't hurt Him.

It hurts us.

When we have pride, it makes us look down on others. It hurts love. It changes relationships. It causes civil wars.

The pride of inflating our person-worth hurts worship, and worship is one of our primary needs and responsibilities.

The Ten Commandments and other commands of God are not just to make us conform to His whims. They are for our good.

He is bright, and knows best.

No Room for Pride

*Who makes you different
from anyone else?*
I Corinthians 4:7

Paul's question is about who colored our skin, who designed our DNA, and who chose our parents.

The people at Corinth were arguing about their favorite leaders in the church, and it was upsetting to Paul, one of the founders: "One of you says, 'I follow Paul'; another, 'I follow Apollos'; another, 'I follow Christ'" (I Corinthians 1:12).

I imagine the last group said their favorite with a very pious sound in their voices.

Paul corrects this for them and us with provocative questions: "What, after all is Apollos? And what is Paul?" (I Corinthians 3:5).

Answer: "Only servants, through whom you came to believe—as the Lord has assigned to each his task.

"I planted the seed, Apollos watered, but God made it grow.... For we are God's fellow workers" (I Corinthians 3:5–9).

Our Differences

God created each of us with purpose. He made us different from each other. (Amazing that two eyes and ears and one nose and one mouth can go together in so many billions of ways that we can recognize each other!)

And He did not make all these differences so we would envy others or be proud of ourselves!

Instead, it is so that we would be grateful!

So the issue is to stop pride and envy.

If you like how I speak or lead, thank you. But don't put me in a contest with others who speak or lead. That is the word from our Creator-Designer.

The pitcher is not more important than the right fielder.

There is no room for either envy or pride in God's family.

Not about others, not about ourselves.

We do not brag or get cocky about gifts—we thank the giver.

God.

Who is not only the source of our gifts, but the ultimate Lord who will judge us for our attitude toward God and His gifts to us.

"It is the Lord who judges me," Paul the apostle wrote (I Corinthians 4:4). He says that to stop people from picking favorites and causing factions.

Can you imagine what government would be like if leaders honored God and their differences with this kind of understanding?

Or where you work?

Shall we talk about family?

Cultural differences?

NO ROOM FOR PRIDE BECAUSE GOD GIFTED US

What do you have
that you did not receive?
I Corinthians 4:7

Jeanine and I spent 26 years of our lives in Akron, Ohio, where there's a bit of self-consciousness because it is not the sunbelt of America or a financial center. Many of us think the area has a bad self-image, in many minds at least.

What a gift it has been to us. Some of the most wonderful people in the world, the most generous, the true "salt of the earth," live there. Its hospitals and schools and many places of work are led by people who care, who seek to be fair and loving, who carry concepts of grace and mercy into the workplace.

Point is, it's easy to live in a nice city like that and still not see all of these good things as gifts from God. That's why I wanted to say it on paper right here, and to not let myself accept the daily good things like that as coincidence. Instead, Paul's words apply even to the daily benefits—"What do you have that you did not receive?"

Gifts are of grace. Our good traits and abilities are gifts from God.

Even our blessings and good fortunes.

He is the giver of all good and perfect gifts (James 1:18).

He is the one who makes us different from each other. He colors our skin. He crosses paths with us and builds our spirits and gives health to our bodies.

Even our abilities and intelligence are gifts, and should promote grateful hearts. Think it through.

Paul asked his friends who were reading this letter—and he asks us who have never met him—where we got the good things we have. What do you have that you did not receive?

Obvious implication—it was a gift. You received it. You did not earn it or manufacture it or whip it up or train yourself into this good gift.

And so we should ask ourselves—what good things, inherent in our DNA or our spiritual treasures, did we make ourselves? Which of us picked our own parents? Which of us were able to mold our personality at the beginning so that we have joy and love and happiness?

Not a soul among us has earned anything about eternity!

But I'm jumping ahead. He wants us to think about what makes us differ from others, because those are things that usually make us proud toward others.

What do you have that you did not receive? And if you received it, why are you proud?

End of lecture in a way.

It was George Herbert who wrote a short prayer we should never forget:

> *Thou who hast given so much,*
> *give one thing more:*
> *a grateful heart.*

YOU DECIDE.

Gift...Gratitude

If the good gifts we have—even the places we live—are from almighty God, the giver of every good and perfect gift, then we should not go around proud but rather grateful.

The implication is clear. I guess the only question is, if we go along with this?

Or will I live my life in pride and think that my gifted nationality or race is better than someone else's?

We rest in the sovereignty of God on other issues, even the worldwide events of history. We like to say that God is going to bring this ship into port at the right time. We believe that even evil will somehow be punished so much that God will be glorified. Even for the wrong that has been done. The Bible says this clearly!

But in this passage we're asked to trust God related to our gifts and our differences.

The blunt question is, "Who makes you to differ from another?"

And the blunt, implied answer is, God. God the sovereign ruler of the universe. God the sovereign dispenser of gifts. God who has been accused of being unfair or who is sometimes criticized because we think He did it the wrong way.

But these verses are asking us to trust Him. And to thank Him. It's clear.

Before we even start on the basics and personal gifts God has given us, think of all the freebies that we easily take for granted. Shall we say air? And how in the world did our lungs get designed so they could use the air to bring oxygen and send it to our blood and...?

"What do you have that you did not receive?"

And especially salvation—not one part of it was earned!

It is the gift of God.

Ephesians explains, "It is by grace you have been saved, through faith—and this not from yourselves, it is the gift of God—not by works, so that no one can boast" (2:8,9).

Looking Down on Others

The context in I Corinthians 4 is very clear. Paul is noting how some people feel so proud about their status and start arguing about who is better. This happens in the church, but it also happens in city council and the P.T.A.

It happens in politics all the time.

Churches look down on others who don't agree with them, or don't have "quite as much truth" as a gift from God!

Check in at your home or office right now—church or synagogue also—and you will see how many tensions and crises are personality conflicts. And so often these are because of cliques and favoritism as they were at Corinth.

Negativism or divisiveness, common as they are, are totally unnecessary!

And so we become a nation of critics, analyzing the plays that others run, and saying what they should have done.

Acting as if God dished out all the good things with us and gave some lesser things to others. As if we deserve our good fortune.

Not one of us does. It is all a gift from God.

The Pain of Life

God is sovereign in all issues of life, but He often gets blamed for only the bad things. I don't even know if He causes bad things—I don't think so. I know He never did anything wrong!

I know from Scripture that to live with recognition of His sovereignty is to not get frustrated at all the pain in life, but rather to get closer to God. We are called to recognize that all good gifts come from above, and that the bad stuff is part of the groaning of creation, as it is called in Romans 8. Ever since the fall of man and woman, there have been dandelions and cancer. Pain in work and birth. Evil natures springing up in all of us.

The first four-letter word you or I ever said was "mine." Now the world is filled with four-letter words that embarrass us. And our minds are filled with thoughts and selfishness—anger, pride, lust—that embarrass us also. We need a Savior.

And all of these evidences of that are not caused by God. In fact, He wants to rescue us from them and in them. He accepts us as part of the fallen world. He raises us up with forgiveness and righteousness as gifts.

And He keeps telling us through His writings that He has given us the good gifts of life. And that we should be grateful.

In bad times, let's just make it through it and ask for His good gift of strength and endurance. That's the best way to live.

If our Bible says anything, it says all this, calling for our immediate attention.

So I can look back now at early pains—divorce of our parents, death of my 14-year-old sister, death of my mother by vicious cancer—and at least know God walked with me.

And my desire for the great day of the future heightened—when Christ returns to make the world as it was meant to be.

He will raise the dead and remake the New Heaven and the New Earth.

It will be good.

And we will be forever grateful.

No Room for Pride because God Gifted Us, and We Should Be Thankful.

And if you did receive it,
why do you boast as if you had not received it?
I Corinthians 4:7

Recently someone asked me what memories I have of advice or directives from my mother—the kind that were repetitive. I had no trouble remembering. If you left the dinner table without saying, "Excuse me and thank you," you were back there saying it. No leeway.

And the habit continues for me.

I simply need to be sure I say it to God regularly. "Excuse me" would be more like, "Please forgive me." And "thank you" would be more like all the time!

He has given us so much!

So what is a life of gratitude? What does it look like to meet someone grateful?

Whether the man or woman is rich or poor, can you tell someone who honors God with gratitude when you meet him or her?

I think so.

I think you can tell because they listen to your words, don't look down on you, don't use sarcasm, and sometimes even express gratitude openly to God.

I think you can tell by the way they treat small children, and people who have much less.

Perhaps we can tell this in our own lives by how we respond to what some people call "little people," sometimes little in stature and age, but sometimes little in holdings.

Their house is small, their car is rusted, and their vocabulary is not as rich.

And instead of being grateful, we walk past them, or wish they wouldn't hold up that sign of need.

We can tell by how often we say thank you to God.

There are other places in the Bible that say we should give thanks always (I Thessalonians 5:18). It is obviously a way of life. A way of kindness. A way of joy.

And the reason we received these gifts is also clear—to serve others.

So the wealth that you have in intellect or even money and especially in spirit—it is not to be for a private party. God invests in us and gives us gifts so we can serve others.

Gratitude produces unselfish service to others in the name of the Lord.

Apology

And here I apologize to those who have been hurt by the church or the pride of believers through the years. I realize I have no position from which to apologize except that I have been in church work for over 40 years and sometimes carried an attitude of pride. I realize I have no office like the superintendent of churches or the president of a council or the pope of the world. But maybe all of us can live with the reminder in our hearts that many believers and many people have been proud instead of grateful, unkind instead of gracious. Together we apologize.

We can change this.

And we can live with a strong attitude of gratitude and grace, thankful for how God has loved us.

There is a fine line between confidence and cockiness. Confidence is the trust we have in Christ as Savior and Lord, assurance that He is true. That He was not playing games. That He was not lying also.

He did claim to be the Son of God. He accepted worship. He said, "Before Abraham was, I AM" (John 8:58).

And He lived a perfect life.

Any questions?

But He didn't go around with a cockiness that some Christians have. As if what we believe makes us better persons, or more reliable to God. Nonsense.

God chooses all of us to be loved and to be offered His grace. He then gives that forgiveness and grace to all who ask, who are willing to admit that they are not good enough on their own.

Sadly, some of them turn around and act like they deserved it, looking down on people who have not asked for such gracious treatment. It's foolish. It's sad.

It calls for another apology.

But what we're saying is that people who receive gifts should simply be grateful. Not proud at all. Not acting like they are above anybody. Living in gratitude.

Some Never Notice

Some people never get very close to gratitude. Not within a mile.

They never look into the gift. They could not even explain what the God of the Bible claims through His writers is the free gift of forgiveness and righteousness.

It's one thing to say you don't believe you can win $3,000,000 by clicking a link on the internet. However, if your neighbors, friends, or fellow worshipers show you the money, you'd be foolish not to got to the site and see for yourself.

Such is life.

Maybe the farthest thing from gratitude is total unbelief, and even the refusal to check it out.

As a follower of Christ, that should not make me angry as much as frustrated and patient. For God is patient with me every day, and with all.

But it does seem important and even intellectually honest to look at the claims of this fantastic Scripture, which has amazing statements about the future. The prophecies did come true or still will.

Grandma

I am grateful that at an early age the nicest person in the world, Grandma Rosa, helped me look into the Bible on a daily basis.

She told us constantly what God had done for us and that He would like to forgive us. That He had a way of walking with us in the daily stuff of life.

Her grammar was not perfect—she had a fourth grade education. Her manners were nothing but kindness. Her appearance was homely—I hesitate to write it but she was not blessed with many physical attributes that some have.

But her heart! Her heart was grateful and kind. She took us to children's Bible classes in the deserted and poverty sections of Harrisburg, crossing racial and financial lines before anyone did. She prayed for us regularly and even sincerely thanked God for the little bit of riches she had.

She modeled thanksgiving. I saw it regularly.

And her faith gave her confidence in the future for sure.

My Change Point

On the day I embraced this verse and belief, I slid to my knees beside my study chair and thanked God. I asked for help to be grateful all my life and never proud about any achievements.

And to realize that what I have and what I am are because of God's love and gifts.

He made me different as He did you. Everything good that I have has been a delivery from God. He has given the gifts.

May I never forget.

You remember what He has given you.

YOU DECIDE.

Epilogue

All of this rises or falls with the one person, Jesus the Christ.

Born by the word of God the Father with the help of a virgin woman, He was two for one whole year.

Normal yet perfect, He grew "in wisdom and stature, and in favor with God and man" (Luke 2:52).

When He fell He skinned His knee and bled. He learned spelling. When He sat in geography He did not raise His hand to say He knew where all the countries are because He put them there.

Jesus was a carpenter, a very good one we assume. His word was good, His character perfect.

He loved people of all kinds, shapes, and sizes. He didn't have to say much about it; He was forever showing it. But He taught about that love too. He said, "I did not come to call the righteous, but sinners" (Matt 9:13).

He told people to love their neighbors, anyone around them, just like they loved themselves (Luke 10:27). And even though His own neighbors rejected Him, yet He loved them. He took time with them.

Children would run to sit on His lap. The lepers had a saying among themselves, "Jesus is one of us." The crippled had hearts that skipped a beat when they saw Him coming. Even when they were not among the ones He healed, He brought courage into their souls. It was not the magic He brought to their muscles—it was the way He touched and talked to them. It was the tenderness they felt in His calloused hands.

Yes, Jesus loves us. It's one of the first songs we learn by heart, and it strengthens our hearts still.

He befriended the herpes carriers, without a thought of falling. He sat down with the winebibbers, but never made a selfish or foolish move. He moved toward people others ran away from. He allowed a streetwalker to wash His feet with her tears, dry them with her hair, and walk quietly away with newfound forgiveness and peace in her heart. "The tax-gatherers and harlots did believe Him " (Matt 21:32).

Friend of sinners, He came for me. Associate of the selfish, He went to the house of Zaccheus for tea, and ended up at mine.

For I was that sinner, and I that crippled fool. I was covered with the leprosy of selfishness and He did not run away, but held my hand.

I was a child of hell, but He adopted me and reassigned my eternity.

I was a mixed-up teenager with pimples on my face and questions on my soul and He taught me how to live.

He lifted me, and for no reason. No, for one reason—love!

Nothing displays His supernatural grace and love like His reaction to those who despised Him. He did not get even, but left that up to His heavenly Father, as should we.

They asked trick questions. He answered graciously, but pointedly. If they were hurting someone else, He stepped in, and stuck their feet in their mouths, as at the time when the hypocritical Pharisees were about to execute a woman caught in immorality. But when it would have been personal revenge, He opened not His mouth.

"Love your enemies," He taught in the Sermon on the Mount. Return good for evil.

When someone slaps you on your cheek, turn to him your other.

And then He got the chance to practice what He preached. They slapped Him on the face, and He prayed for them. They gouged His eyes, and He cried for them.

He was tied to a slab and whipped on the back in the vicious Roman manner, and He endured with patience.

They pulled out His beard whiskers with wooden pliers and He did not call down angels to the rescue.

They (in a sense, we were all there) got a crowd to sway from its Palm Sunday admiration and call for His death, all the time mocking His lack of power to stop the sideshow.

They laughed at His "weakness," as they labeled it, and smashed thorns deeply into His throbbing forehead. They spit in His face, yet He remained calm.

They put Him through the mockery of a trial, fixed and fraudulent, and He endured. "Thou sayest," He said when asked if He was God, admitting He was truth.

They killed Him, not in a quick extermination, but in the cruelest and most humiliating of tortures, "even the death on the cross." He would leave a cup of juice and a piece of bread so we would never forget.

He was marched through the alleyways of Jerusalem as an exhibit of Roman victory. Carrying a heavy cross, He was whipped again.

They say the beauty of a man's character comes out under pressure. Here were all the physical, emotional, mental, social, and spiritual forces pushing against one person all alone, and His character was only holy, His response only loving.

His enemies hammered spikes into His wrists and ankles, and hung Him, naked, to an upright cross, where He was jeered by the soldiers and the crowd.

He only responded, "Father, forgive them—they know not what they do."

In the hell that He faced, He showed that He is heaven.

His death for all of us was followed, three days later, by the greatest event since creation.

He arose from the dead. He broke the chains of the grave.

And He promises the same for all who hang on to Him by faith.

He has changed and is changing my heart, and would like to do the same for you.

YOU DECIDE.